Caitlin Courtney's
Books

# EARLY MOON

I AM CHICAGO

# EARLY MOON

## BY CARL SANDBURG

ILLUSTRATED BY JAMES DAUGHERTY

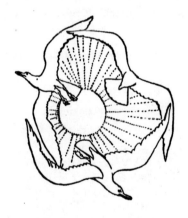

## OFFICE

A VOYAGER/HBJ BOOK

HARCOURT BRACE JOVANOVICH

NEW YORK AND LONDON

Printed in the United States of America

Library of Congress Cataloging in Publication Data
Sandburg, Carl, 1878–1967.
Early moon.

(A Voyager/HBJ book)
SUMMARY: An anthology by a well-known American poet grouped under such topical headings as "Wind and Sea," "Portraits," and "Birds and Bugs."
[1. American poetry] I. Daugherty, James Henry, 1889–1974. II. Title.
PS3537.A618E3    1978    811'.5'2    77-16488
ISBN 0-15-627326-8

First Voyager/HBJ edition 1978

A   B   C   D   E   F   G   H   I   J

HBJ

The courtesy of Holt, Rinehart and Winston, Inc., is hereby acknowledged for permission to reprint the following poems from volumes copyrighted by them: from *Cornhuskers*— "Early Moon," "Laughing Corn," "Psalm of Those Who Go Forth Before Daylight," "Upstairs," "Baby Face," "Illinois Farmer," "Chicago Poet," "Prayers of Steel," "Street Windows"; from *Chicago Poems*—"Sketch," "Lost," "Happiness," "Fog," "Theme in Yellow," "Fish Crier," "Young Sea," "Child Moon," "To Beachey."

# CONTENTS

9

## BIRDS AND BUGS

## NIGHT

11

# SHORT TALK ON POETRY

*with different kinds of explanations for young
people as to how little anybody knows about
poetry, how it is made, what it is made of, how
long men have been making it, where it came
from, when it began, who started it and why,
and who knows all about it.*

WHAT is poetry? Is the answer hidden somewhere? Is it one of those answers locked in a
box and nobody has the key? There are such
questions and answers.

Once a man reading a newspaper clipped a poem written by a small boy in a school in New York City. The
lines read:

> There stands the elephant.
> Bold and strong—
> There he stands chewing his food.
> We are strengthless against his strength.

And the man has kept this poem for many years. He
has a feeling the boy did a good, honest piece of writing.
The boy stood wondering and thinking before the biggest
four-legged animal on earth today. And the boy put his

wonder and thought, his personal human secret, a touch of man's fear in the wilderness, into the nineteen words of the poem. He asked, "What does the elephant do to me when I look at him? What is my impression of the elephant?" Then he answered his own questions.

Once there was a boy went to school and learned that any two-legged animal is a biped. And he said, "Here I've been a biped all the time and I didn't know it." So there are people sometimes who talk poetry without writing it but they don't know they are talking poetry. And every child, every boy and girl, sometimes has poetry in his head and heart—even though it doesn't get written.

Once there was a wee, curly-headed boy tugged at a cornstalk, tugged till he pulled the cornstalk up all by himself and told about it to his father, who said, "I guess you're getting to be a pretty strong boy now." The little one answered, "I guess I am. The whole earth had a hold of the other end of the cornstalk and was pulling against me." Should we say this boy had imagination and what he told his father was so keen and alive it could be called poetry? Perhaps he was a poet without knowing it just like the boy who was a biped without knowing it.

Poetry is old, ancient, goes far back. It is among the oldest of human things. So old is it that no man knows how and why the first poems came.

When it shall happen sometime that men gather their gifts and go to work and write a history of language, then it may be that we shall have at the same time a history of poetry. For the first poems of man probably came about the same time the first men, women and children spoke the first human words on the earth.

Is any one surprised to hear that we do not have a history of poetry? Shall we believe that the learned men have written histories of all the important things of mankind? Surely there are many big histories yet to be written on big subjects. We do not have, for instance, a history of Money that goes back to when money first began, telling how and why. We do not have a history of Language which goes far back, telling how and why men first began to talk.

Yes, poetry is old. The first men that walked the earth, before men had learned to write, must have talked poetry to each other sometimes. Among the oldest things we have today which tell us about the Indians, the Chinese, the Egyptians, how they lived and talked, thousands of years ago, are writings we know to be poetry. These writings have words that go along with timebeats, with rhythm, one-two, one-two, or one-two-three-four, one-two-three-four. They had drums among the Indians, the Chinese, the Egyptians, thousands of years ago. And the words of their poetry move along like drum-beats, keeping time, now fast, now slow, drumming easy and slow at the opening of a war dance, drumming faster and faster, wild and furious, till it is so swift only the best-trained warriors can stand the speed of the dance that is drummed.

We have old poems, some so old no man knows how far they go back in time. One beautiful ancient English poem has no author, whose name we know. Where it came from no history books tell us. It goes like this—

On a misty moisty morning, when cloudy was the
    weather,
I chanced to meet an old man all clothed in leather.
He began to compliment and I began to grin,
"How do you do? and how do you do? and how do you
    do again?"

This is only one of many fine and strange poems we have out of the long ago. Nobody knows who wrote them or whether they were first spoken centuries before they were written down to meet our eyes in books.

What is poetry? This question no man has ever answered in such a way that all men have said, "Yes, now we know what poetry is." Many men have tried to explain what poetry is. Some men have written thick books so the question might be settled and made clear for all time. But they have all failed. Several fine poets have written essays and papers on what they believe poetry to be. Yet these poets did not do what they started out to do. They meant to explain in prose what poetry is and they ended up with writing poetry to explain poetry.

This is like a man inside of a strange house trying to tell people outside who have never been in the house exactly how it feels to be in that house, which is not scientific nor exact and which is like saying, "The way to write poems is to write poems." It is only clear and understandable to those who already understand and therefore need no explanations.

When Walt Whitman says, "The poet is the answerer," we are interested. If we could know just what he means by "the answerer" we would know what he means by "the poet." One poet says poetry must be "cold, lonely and distant," not knowing that some readers of poetry are glad to have books which are warm, friendly and so near that they almost breathe with life. Another poet has said poetry is "emotion remembered in tranquillity." What does that mean? It is anybody's guess what that means. To know exactly what it means we would have to know exactly what is emotion, what is tranquillity, and what we do when we remember. Otherwise it is an escape from words into words, "passing the buck," or winding like a weasel through language that ends about where it begins. "He came out of the same hole he went in at."

There is a science called "esthetics." It is the science which tries to find the laws of beauty. If as a science it ever became perfect then the books dealing with that science would become very important. Then when a builder finished a house and wished to know whether it was a beautiful house he would only have to open the books on esthetics and the books would tell him.

What is beauty? And when shall we call a thing beautiful? These, too, are questions no man has ever answered in such a way that all men have said, "Yes, now we know what beauty is and now we know how to tell the beautiful when we find it." The nearest that men have come to answering the question, "What is the beautiful?" has been in their saying the beautiful is *the appropriate*, that which serves. No hat is a beautiful hat which does not fit you and which the wind can easily blow off your head. A Five-gallon Hat on a cowboy riding a horse on an Arizona ranch is beautiful—but the same hat on a crowded city street car would be out of place, inappropriate. No song is beautiful in a room where persons desire complete quiet. No polite behavior has beauty unless it has thought and consideration for others. The most beautiful room is the one which best serves those who live in it.

The most beautiful skyscrapers are those without extras stuck on after the real structure is finished. Why should a good, honest skyscraper have a dome or a mosque or a cement wedding cake plastered on top of it? Nearly always, what serves, what is appropriate to human use, is beautiful enough—without extras. A farm silo, a concrete grain elevator, a steel barge hauling iron ore on the Great Lakes, or a series of tall coal chutes rising as silhouettes on a moonlight night, may any one of them have as complete a beauty as the Greek Parthenon or a Gothic cathedral. Steichen, the photographer, declares he occasionally meets newspaper photographs which in design and as works of art are superior to many of the proclaimed masterpieces of painting and etching.

Now, poetry is supposed to be the esthetic art which gathers the beautiful into words. The first stuff for making poetry is words. No poems, strictly speaking, have ever been made without words. To make poems without words would be like a painter painting without paint or a bricklayer bricklaying without bricks. Of course, a feeling or a thought, or both must come to a poet before he begins using the words that make a poem. But the right words, the special and particular words for the purpose in view, these must come. For out of them the poem is made.

The words for a poem sometimes come swiftly and easily so that at last when the poem is put down on paper, the writer of them says, "I do not know how these words came. What is here was not my own absolute doing any more than a dream that should come to me in a night of sleep." Yet again the words may come slowly, out of years of toil and sometimes anguish of changing phrases and arrangements.

While we do not know very much in an absolute way about the questions, "What is poetry? How is a poem made?" we do know the one little fact that poems are made of words and without words there can be no poetry. Beyond this we do not know much. However, there is one other little scientific fact we know about poetry. That is, what is poetry for any given individual depends on the individual and what his personality requires as poetry. This links up with one of the few accepted propositions of the science of esthetics: Beauty depends on personal taste. What is beauty for one person is not for another. What is poetry for one person may be balderdash or hogwash for another.

Each of us has a personality different from all others. It has even been said that as no two leaves in a forest are the same no two human characters are precisely alike. This personality that each of us has is strangely woven of millions of little facts, events, impressions out of the past and present. Your personality and mine go back to many mysterious human connections before we were born— and since. And what any one of us loves today with depth of passion, and what each of us tries to shape his life by, goes back to strange things in personality, things so darkly mixed and baffling that it is not easy for any of us at a given time to answer the question, "Why do you love this and not that? Why do you want those and not them?" The old song with its line, "I want what I want when I want it," is not entirely comic in its backgrounds.

We do not know the start of the old folk saying, "Every one to his taste as the old woman said when she kissed the cow." We are sure a blunt Indiana philosopher knew his ground well when he wrote, "What is one man's lettuce is another man's poison ivy." These are humorous comments on the deeply serious and involved reality known as human personality. They connect directly with the fact that what is poetry for some is not poetry for others. They indicate that sometimes we cannot help it that we do not merely *dislike* some poetry; we go farther and *hate* it. And why we should hate any particular poem, thing or person is no more clear than why we love others, for hate is usually expensive in many ways and is a waste of time that belongs elsewhere. Charles Lamb said he believed an old story he had heard about two men, who had never before seen each other, meeting one day in a street in London—and the moment they saw each other's faces they leaped and began fighting.

Lamb said those two men who began hitting at each other's faces the moment they saw those faces, had "imperfect sympathies." Something clicked in each one saying, "Hit him! Kill him!" They couldn't help it. Though they met in a crowded street of a great city, and there was no war on, they attacked each other like two soldiers with bayonets in front line trenches.

And exactly like those two men meeting in a London street, some of us register instantly—though not so violently—to faces we meet, buildings, colors, neckties, gowns, designs, pictures, books, plays—and poems. Something clicks in us and we know like a flash whether we like this or that new thing we meet for the first time.

And then may happen afterward a slow change of our viewpoint. What we saw nothing in to begin with takes on a glint or two we had not noticed at first; then as time passes, we gather values, intentions, gleams, that interest us and lead us on till we know we were ignorant, possessed of "imperfect sympathies," in our first impression of hate or dislike. This change of viewpoint from dislike to interest, from indifference to enthusiasm, often has happened with the finest of men and women in respect to great masterpieces of literature. Sometimes we do not know what a writer is talking about in his books because in life we have not met the people, facts, impressions which he is trying to deliver his mind and heart about in his book. Said a great modern artist, "Going along a railroad one day I see a thing I have seen many times. But this day I suddenly *see*. 'Tisn't that you *see* new, but things have prepared you for *a new vision*."

As the years pass by and experience writes out new records in our mind life, we go back to some works of art that we rejected in the early days and find values we missed. Work, love, laughter, pain, death, put impressions on us as time passes, and as we brood over what has happened.

Out of songs and scars and the mystery of personal development, we get eyes that pick out intentions we had not seen before in people, in works of art, in books and poetry.

Naturally, too, the reverse happens. What we register to at one period of life, what we find gay and full of fine nourishment at one time, we find later has lost interest for us. A few masterpieces may last across the years but we usually discard some. A few masterpieces are enough. Why this is so we do not know. For each individual his new acquisitions and old discards are different.

The books and poems at hand ready for each of us are so many and so different that we use and throw away, acquire and discard, according to personal taste, and often merely guided by whim like the man in the song, "I want what I want when I want it." Too often both among young people and grownups, there is a careless drifting and they take the easiest way in books and poetry. Millions read without asking themselves why they read and whether in all their reading they have learned anything worth the spending of their time.

It was not for nothing Thoreau said an old newspaper would do for him just as well as a new one. Each of us can sit alone with our conscience for a while on the proposition of Robert Louis Stevenson that the intelligent man can find an Iliad of the human race in a newspaper. And any kindly philosopher could write a thick book on why the shrewd, tolerant reader enjoys even a stupid, vain, hypocritical book because the writer of the book is etching his own portrait on every page, stepping forth and talking off lines like one of the fools, clowns or pretenders in a Russian play. Healthy questions for each of us: "Why do I read books? What do books do to me? Can I improve my form as a reader? What does poetry do to me? Why do I need this or that poetry?"

We have heard much in our time about free verse being modern, as though it is a new-found style for men to use in speaking and writing, rising out of the machine age, skyscrapers, high speed and jazz. Now, if free verse is a form of writing poetry without rime, without regular meters, without established and formal rules governing it, we can easily go back to the earliest styles of poetry known to the human family—and the style is strictly free verse. Before men invented the alphabet, so that poems could be put down in writing, they spoke their poems. When one man spoke to another in a certain timebeat and rhythm, if it happened that his words conveyed certain impressions and moods to his listeners, he was delivering poetry to them, whether he knew it or they knew it, and whether he or they had a name for an art which the poet was practicing on himself and them.

We may go through thousands of pages of the reports of songs, poems and spoken dreams of American Indians as recorded in the volumes of the Bureau of Ethnology of the Smithsonian Institution at Washington, and we find it all to be in the free verse style. The poems of the ancient Chinese writers Li Po, Tu Fu and others, as read in translations, and as notated by the translators, show how strange and marvelous moments of life can be captured and compressed in the manner called free verse. The Bible is one of the sublime sources of free verse. The orations of Moses, the Book of Proverbs, Ecclesiastes, the Sermon on the Mount, the "love chapter" of the Apostle Paul, these are in the free verse style of writing poetry.

If those who write in the free verse style fail at getting onto paper any lines worth reading twice, they are in the same class with those who in regular, ordered, formal verse fail to get onto paper lines worth reading twice. The crimes of free verse have been many. The same goes for sonnets, ballads, ballades, triolets, rondeaus, villanelles, and the forms of verse which are governed by hexameters, pentameters, iambics, strophes and by laws which dictate how many syllables shall be permitted to perch on each line of the poem.

Perhaps no wrong is done and no temple of human justice violated in pointing out here that each authentic poet makes a style of his own. Sometimes this style is so clearly the poet's own that when he is imitated it is known who is imitated. Shakespeare, Villon, Li Po, Whitman—each sent forth his language and impress of thought and feeling from a different style of gargoyle spout. In the spacious highways of great books each poet is allowed the stride that will get him where he wants to go.

Should children write poetry? Yes, whenever they feel like it. If nothing else happens they will find it a training for writing and speaking in other fields of human work and play. No novelist has been a worse writer for having practiced at poetry. Many a playwright, historian, essayist, editorial writer, could have improved his form by experimenting with poetry.

At what age should a child begin writing poetry? Any age. Poems are made of words and when a child is learning to talk, to shape words on its tongue, is a proper time for it to speak poetry—if it can.

Does it help a child poet to have praise for his poems? The child should be told that poetry is first of all for the poet, that great poets usually die saying their best work is not written. Perhaps it is wise for every child to be told that it is a mistake for either a child or a grown-up accomplished artist to be satisfied with any past performance.

The foremost American woman poet, Emily Dickinson, had scarcely any of her poetry published in her lifetime. What she wrote had to be. And it is doubtful if her poems would have had the same complete glory they have if she had been taken up and praised. On the other hand there have been poets saved to live and write beautiful pages because they found friends, an audience, and enough money to keep the wolf from sniffing round their little doorways.

The father of a great Irish poet once remarked, "What can be explained is not poetry." There are people who want a book of verse to be like the arithmetic—you turn to the back of the book and find the answers. Ken Nakazawa notes, "The poems that are obvious are like the puzzles that are already solved. They deny us the joy of seeking and creating."

Once a little girl showed to a friend a poem she had written. "Why didn't you make it longer?" asked the friend. "I could have," she answered, "but then it wouldn't have been a poem." She meant she left something in the air for the reader of the poem to linger over, as any of us do over a rose or a sunset or a face. Roses, sunsets, faces, have mystery. If we could explain them, then after having delivered our explanations we could say, "Take it from me, that's all there is to it, and there's no use your going any further for I've told you all there is and there isn't any more."

If poems could be explained, then poets would have to leave out roses, sunsets, faces, from their poems. Yet it seems that for thousands of years poets have been writing about roses, sunsets, faces, because they have mystery, significance, and a heavy or a light beauty, an appeal, a lesson and a symbolism that stays with us long as we live. It was something like this in the heart of the philosopher who declared, "What can be explained is not poetry."

# PICTURES OF TODAY

## POTOMAC TOWN IN FEBRUARY

The bridge says: Come across, try me; see how good I
am.

The big rock in the river says: Look at me; learn how
to stand up.

The white water says: I go on; around, under, over, I
go on.

A kneeling, scraggly pine says: I am here yet; they
nearly got me last year.

A sliver of moon slides by on a high wind calling: I know
why; I'll see you tomorrow; I'll tell you everything
tomorrow.

# PEOPLE WHO MUST

I painted on the roof of a skyscraper.
I painted a long while and called it a day's work.
The people on a corner swarmed and the traffic cop's
    whistle never let up all afternoon.
They were the same as bugs, many bugs on their way—
Those people on the go or at a standstill;
And the traffic cop a spot of blue, a splinter of brass,
Where the black tides ran around him
And he kept the street. I painted a long while
And called it a day's work.

## SKY PIECES

Proudly the fedoras march on the heads of the some-
what careless men.

Proudly the slouches march on the heads of the still
more careless men.

Proudly the panamas perch on the noggins of dapper
debonair men.

Comically somber the derbies gloom on the earnest sol-
emn noodles.

And the sombrero, most proud, most careless, most dapper and debonair of all, somberly the sombrero
marches on the heads of important men who know
what they want.

Hats are sky-pieces; hats have a destiny; wish your hat
slowly; your hat is you.

## NEW FARM TRACTOR

Snub nose, the guts of twenty mules are in your cylin-
ders and transmission.

The rear axles hold the kick of twenty Missouri jack-
asses.

It is in the records of the patent office and the ads there
is twenty horse power pull here.

The farm boy says hello to you instead of twenty mules
—he sings to you instead of ten span of mules.

A bucket of oil and a can of grease is your hay and oats.

Rain proof and fool proof they stable you anywhere in
the fields with the stars for a roof.

I carve a team of long ear mules on the steering wheel
—it's good-by now to leather reins and the songs
of the old mule skinners.

# DAN

Early May, after cold rain the sun baffling cold wind.
Irish setter pup finds a corner near the cellar door, all
    sun and no wind,
Cuddling there he crosses forepaws and lays his skull
Sideways on this pillow, dozing in a half-sleep,
Browns of hazel nut, mahogany, rosewood, played off
    against each other on his paws and head.

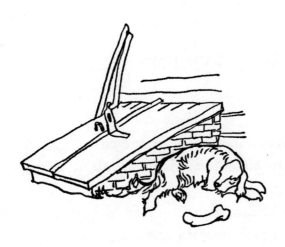

## EVEN NUMBERS

### I

A house like a man all lean and coughing,
a man with his two hands in the air at a cry,
"Hands up."
A house like a woman shrunken and stoop-shouldered,
shrunken and done with dishes and dances.
These two houses I saw going uphill in Cincinnati.

### II

Two houses leaning against each other like drunken
brothers at a funeral,

Two houses facing each other like two blind wrestlers
hunting a hold on each other,
These four scrawny houses I saw on a dead level
cinder patch in Scranton, Pennsylvania.

### III

And by the light of a white moon in Waukesha, Wis-
consin,
I saw a lattice work in lilac time . . . white-mist lavender
. . . a sweet moonlit lavender . . .

# SLOW PROGRAM

The iron rails run into the sun.
The setting of the sun chooses an hour.
The red rail ribbons run into the red ball sun.
The ribbons and the ball change like red water lights.
The picture floats with a slow program of red haze lights.

## PHIZZOG

This face you got,
This here phizzog you carry around,
You never picked it out for yourself, at all, at all—did
　　you?
This here phizzog—somebody handed it to you—am I
　　right?
Somebody said, "Here's yours, now go see what you can
　　do with it."
Somebody slipped it to you and
　　it was like a package marked:
"No goods exchanged after
　　being taken away"—
This face you got.

## AGAIN?

Old Man Woolworth put up a building.
There it was; his dream; all true;
The biggest building in the world.
Babel, the Nineveh Hanging Gardens,
Karnak, all old, outclassed.
And now, here at last, what of it?
What about it? Well, every morning
We'll walk around it and look up.
And every morning we'll ask what
It means and where it's going.
It's a dream; all true; going somewhere,
That's a cinch; women buying mousetraps,
Wire cloth dishrags, ten cent sheet music,
They paid for it; the electric tower

Might yell an electric sign to the inbound
Ocean liners, "Look what the washerwomen
Of America can do with their nickels," or
"See what a nickel and a dime can do,"

And that wouldn't clear Old Man Woolworth's
Head; it was a mystery, a dream, the biggest
Building in the world; Babel, the Nineveh
Hanging Gardens, Karnak, all old,
Outclassed. So the old man cashes in,
The will of the old man is dug out,
And the widow gets thirty million dollars,
Enough to put up another building,
Another bigger than any in the world,
Bigger than Babel, the Nineveh Hanging Gardens,
Karnak, another mystery, another dream
To stand and look up at
And ask what it means.

## BUFFALO DUSK

The buffaloes are gone.
And those who saw the buffaloes are gone.
Those who saw the buffaloes by thousands and how they
    pawed the prairie sod into dust with their hoofs,
    their great heads down pawing on in a great pageant
    of dusk,
Those who saw the buffaloes are gone.
And the buffaloes are gone.

## PLUNGER

Empty the last drop.
Pour out the final clinging heartbeat.
Great losers look on and smile.
Great winners look on and smile.

Plunger:
Take a long breath and let yourself go.

# CHILDREN

## CHILD MOON

The child's wonder
At the old moon
Comes back nightly.
She points her finger
To the far silent yellow thing
Shining through the branches
Filtering on the leaves a golden sand,
Crying with her little tongue, "See the moon!"
And in her bed fading to sleep
With babblings of the moon on her little mouth.

## UPSTAIRS

I too have a garret of old playthings.
I have tin soldiers with broken arms upstairs.
I have a wagon and the wheels gone upstairs.
I have guns and a drum, a jumping-jack and a magic
    lantern.
And dust is on them and I never look at them upstairs.
I too have a garret of old playthings.

# WINTER MILK

The milk drops on your chin, Helga,
Must not interfere with the cranberry red of your cheeks
Nor the sky winter blue of your eyes.
Let your mammy keep hands off the chin.
This is a high holy spatter of white on the reds and blues.

Before the bottle was taken away,
Before you so proudly began today
Drinking your milk from the rim of a cup
They did not splash this high holy white on your chin.

There are dreams in your eyes, Helga.
Tall reaches of wind sweep the clear blue.
The winter is young yet, so young.
Only a little cupful of winter has touched your lips.
Drink on . . . milk with your lips . . . dreams with
your eyes.

# FIVE CENT BALLOONS

Pietro has twenty red and blue balloons on a string.
They flutter and dance pulling Pietro's arm.
A nickel apiece is what they sell for.

Wishing children tag Pietro's heels.

He sells out and goes the streets alone.

## BABY TOES

There is a blue star, Janet,
Fifteen years' ride from us,
If we ride a hundred miles an hour.

There is a white star, Janet,
Forty years' ride from us,
If we ride a hundred miles an hour.

Shall we ride
To the blue star
Or the white star?

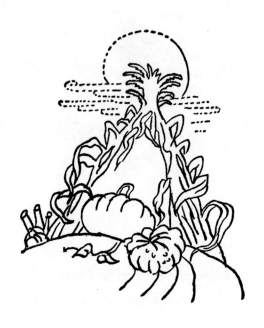

## THEME IN YELLOW

I spot the hills
With yellow balls in autumn.
I light the prairie cornfields
Orange and tawny gold clusters
And I am called pumpkins.
On the last of October
When dusk is fallen
Children join hands
And circle round me
Singing ghost songs

And love to the harvest moon;
I am a jack-o'-lantern
With terrible teeth
And the children know
I am fooling.

# HELGA

The wishes on this child's mouth
Came like snow on marsh cranberries;
The tamarack kept something for her;
The wind is ready to help her shoes.
The north has loved her; she will be
A grandmother feeding geese on frosty
Mornings; she will understand
Early snow on the cranberries
Better and better then.

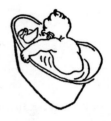

## SLIPPERY

The six month child
Fresh from the tub
Wriggles in our hands.
This is our fish child.
Give her a nickname: Slippery.

## BABY FACE

White Moon comes in on a baby face.
The shafts across her bed are flimmering.

Out on the land White Moon shines,
Shines and glimmers against gnarled shadows,
All silver to slow twisted shadows
Falling across the long road that runs from the house.

Keep a little of your beauty
And some of your flimmering silver
For her by the window tonight
Where you come in, White Moon.

# PRIMER LESSON

Look out how you use proud words.
When you let proud words go, it is not easy to call them
    back.
They wear long boots, hard boots; they walk off proud;
    they can't hear you calling—
Look out how you use proud words.

# WIND AND SEA

## YOUNG SEA

The sea is never still.
It pounds on the shore
Restless as a young heart,
Hunting.

The sea speaks
And only the stormy hearts
Know what it says:
It is the face
of a rough mother speaking.

The sea is young.
One storm cleans all the hoar
And loosens the age of it.
I hear it laughing, reckless.

They love the sea,
Men who ride on it
And know they will die
Under the salt of it

Let only the young come,
     says the sea.
Let them kiss my face
And hear me.

I am the last word
     And I tell
Where storms and
          stars come
          from.

# I AM CHICAGO

*from* THE WINDY CITY

The lean hands of wagon men
put out pointing fingers here,
picked this crossway, put it on a map,
set up their sawbucks, fixed their shotguns,
found a hitching place for the pony express,
made a hitching place for the iron horse,
the one-eyed horse with the fire-spit head,
found a homelike spot and said, "Make a home,"
saw this corner with a mesh of rails, shuttling people,
    shunting cars, shaping the junk of the earth to a
    new city.

The hands of men took hold and tugged
And the breaths of men went into the junk
And the junk stood up into skyscrapers and asked:
Who am I? Am I a city? And if I am what is my name?
And once while the time whistles blew and blew again
The men answered: Long ago we gave you a name,
Long ago we laughed and said: You? Your name is
    Chicago.

Early the red men gave a name to a river,
    the place of the skunk,
    the river of the wild onion smell,
    Shee-caw-go.

Out of the payday songs of steam shovels,
Out of the wages of structural iron rivets,
The living lighted skyscrapers tell it now as a name,
Tell it across miles of sea blue water, gray blue land:
I am Chicago, I am a name given out by the breaths of
    working men, laughing men, a child, a belonging.

So between the Great Lakes,
The Grand De Tour, and the Grand Prairie,
The living lighted skyscrapers stand,
Spotting the blue dusk with checkers of yellow,
    streamers of smoke and silver,
    parallelograms of night-gray watchmen,
Singing a soft moaning song: I am a child, a belonging.

Winds of the Windy City, come out of the prairie, all
    the way from Medicine Hat.
Come out of the inland sea blue water, come where they
    nickname a city for you.

Corn wind in the fall, come off the black lands, come
    off the whisper of the silk hangers, the lap of the
    flat spear leaves.

66

Blue water wind in summer, come off the blue miles of·
lake, carry your inland sea blue fingers, carry us
cool, carry your blue to our homes.

White spring winds, come off the bag wool clouds, come
off the running melted snow, come white as the
arms of snow-born children.

Gray fighting winter winds, come along on the tearing
blizzard tails, the snouts of the hungry hunting
storms, come fighting gray in winter.

Winds of the Windy City,
Winds of corn and sea blue,
Spring wind white and fighting winter gray,
Come home here—they nickname a city for you.

The wind of the lake shore waits and wanders.
The heave of the shore wind hunches the sand piles.
The winkers of the morning stars count out cities
And forget the numbers.

# LOST

Desolate and lone
All night on the lake
Where fog trails and mist creeps,
The whistle of a boat
Calls and cries unendingly,
Like some lost child
In tears and trouble
Hunting the harbor's breast
And the harbor's eyes.

## WIND HORSES

Roots, go deep: wrap your coils; fasten your knots:
Fix a loop far under, a four-in-hand far under:
The wind drives wild horses, gnashers, plungers:
    Go deep, roots.
Hold your four-in-hand knots against all wild horses.

# SAND SCRIBBLINGS

The wind stops, the wind begins.
The wind says stop, begin.

A sea shovel scrapes the sand floor.
The shovel changes, the floor changes.

The sandpipers, maybe they know.
Maybe a three-pointed foot can tell.
Maybe the fog moon they fly to, guesses.

The sandpipers cheep "Here" and get away.
Five of them fly and keep together flying.

Night hair of some sea woman
Curls on the sand when the sea leaves
The salt tide without a good-by.

Boxes on the beach are empty.
Shake 'em and the nails loosen.
They have been somewhere.

# SEA SLANT

On up the sea slant,
On up the horizon,
This ship limps.

The bone of her nose fog-gray,
The heart of her sea-strong,
She came a long way,
She goes a long way.

On up the horizon,
On up the sea-slant,
She limps sea-strong, fog-gray.

She is a green-lit night gray
She comes and goes in the sea fog.
Up the horizon slant she limps.

# SKETCH

The shadows of the ships
Rock on the crest
In the low blue luster
Of the tardy and the soft inrolling tide.

A long brown bar at the dip of the sky
Puts an arm of sand in the span of salt.

The lucid and endless wrinkles
Draw in, lapse and withdraw.
Wavelets crumble and white spent bubbles
Wash on the floor of the beach.

Rocking on the crest
In the low blue luster
Are the shadows of the ships.

# FOG

The fog comes
on little cat feet.

It sits looking
over harbor and city
on silent haunches
and then moves on.

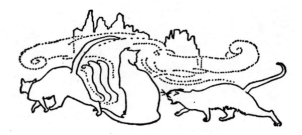

# SANDPIPERS

Ten miles of flat land along the sea.
Sandland where the salt water kills the
    sweet potatoes.
Homes for sandpipers—the script of their
    feet is on the sea shingles—they write
    in the morning, it is gone at noon—
    they write at noon, it is gone at night.
Pity the land, the sea, the ten mile flats,
    pity anything but the sandpiper's
    wire legs and feet.

## SEA-WASH

The sea-wash never ends.
The sea-wash repeats, repeats.
Only old songs? Is that all the sea knows?
    Only the old strong songs?
    Is that all?
The sea-wash repeats, repeats.

# BITTER SUMMER THOUGHTS

The riders of the wind
Weave their shadows,
Trample their time-beats,
Take their time-bars,
Shake out scrolls,
And run over the oats, the barley,
Over the summer wheat-fields.

The farmer and the horse,
The steel and the wagon
Come and clean the fields
And leave us stubble.
The time-bars of the wind are gone;
The shadows, time-beats, scrolls,
They are woven away, put past,
Into the hands of threshers,
Into chaff, into dust,
Into rust and buff of straw stacks,
Into sliding, shoveling oats and wheat.
Over the wheat-fields,
Over the oats,
Summer weaves, is woven away, put past,
Into dust, into rust and buff.

Indian runners ran along this river-road.
They cleaned the wind they clutched in ribs and lungs,
Up over the clean ankles, the clean elbows.
The Frenchmen came with lessons and prayers.
The Scotchmen came with horses and rifles.
Cities, war, railroads came.

In the rain-storms, in the blizzards,
This river-road is clean.

# PORTRAITS

## WINTER WEATHER

It is cold.
The bitter of the winter
whines a story.
It is the colder weather when the truck
drivers sing it would freeze the whiskers
off a brass monkey.
It is the bitterest whining of the winter now.

Well, we might sit down now, have a cup of coffee
apiece, and talk about the weather.

We might look back on things that happened long
ago, times when the weather was different.
Or we might talk about things ahead of us, funny
things in the days, days, days to come, days when
the weather will be different again.

Yes, a cup of coffee apiece.
Even if this winter weather is bitter,
The truck drivers are laughing:
It would freeze the whiskers off a brass monkey.

## MYSTERIOUS BIOGRAPHY

Christofo Colombo was a hungry man,
hunted himself half way round the world;
he began poor, panhandled, ended in jail,
Christofo so hungry, Christofo so poor,
Christofo in the chilly, steel bracelets,
honorable distinguished Christofo Colombo.

# FISH CRIER

I know a Jew fish crier down on Maxwell Street with a
  voice like a north wind blowing over corn stubble
  in January.
He dangles herring before prospective customers evinc-
  ing a joy identical with that of Pavlowa dancing.
His face is that of a man terribly glad to be selling fish,
  terribly glad that God made fish, and customers to
  whom he may call his wares from a pushcart.

## JAZZ FANTASIA

Drum on your drums, batter on your banjos,
sob on the long cool winding saxophones.
Go to it, O jazzmen.

Sling your knuckles on the bottoms of the happy
tin pans, let your trombones ooze, and go husha-
husha-hush with the slippery sand-paper.

Moan like an autumn wind high in the lonesome tree-
tops, moan soft like you wanted somebody terrible,

cry like a racing car slipping away from a motorcycle cop, bang-bang! you jazzmen, bang altogether drums, traps, banjos, horns, tin cans—make two people fight on the top of a stairway and scratch each other's eyes in a clinch tumbling down the stairs.

Can the rough stuff . . . now a Mississippi steamboat pushes up the night river with a hoo-hoo-hoo-oo . . . and the green lanterns calling to the high soft stars . . . a red moon rides on the humps of the low river hills . . . go to it, O jazzmen.

## TO BEACHEY, 1912

Riding against the east,
A veering, steady shadow
Purrs the motor-call
Of the man-bird
Ready with the death-laughter
In his throat
And in his heart always
The love of the big blue beyond.

Only a man,
A far fleck of shadow on the east,

Sitting at ease
With his hands on a wheel
And around him the large gray wings.
Hold him, great soft wings,
Keep and deal kindly, O wings,
With the cool, calm shadow at the wheel.

## WEEDS

From the time of the early radishes
To the time of the standing corn
Sleepy Henry Hackerman hoes.

There are laws in the village against weeds.
The law says a weed is wrong and shall be killed.
The weeds say life is a white and lovely thing
And the weeds come on and on in irrepressible regiments.
Sleepy Henry Hackerman hoes; and the village law ut-
    tering a ban on weeds is unchangeable law.

## STREET WINDOW

The pawn-shop man knows hunger,
And how far hunger has eaten the heart
Of one who comes with an old keepsake.
Here are wedding rings and baby bracelets,
Scarf pins and shoe buckles, jeweled garters,
Old-fashioned knives with inlaid handles,
Watches of old gold and silver,
Old coins worn with finger-marks.
They tell stories.

# ILLINOIS FARMER

Bury this old Illinois farmer with respect.
He slept the Illinois nights of his life after days of work
    in Illinois cornfields.
Now he goes on a long sleep.
The wind he listened to in the cornsilk and the tassels,
    the wind that combed his red beard zero mornings
    when the snow lay white on the yellow ears in the
    bushel basket at the corncrib,
The same wind will now blow over the place here where
    his hands must dream of Illinois corn.

# CHICAGO POET

I saluted a nobody.
I saw him in a looking-glass.
He smiled—so did I.
He crumpled the skin on his forehead,
    frowning—so did I.
Everything I did he did.
I said, "Hello, I know you."
And I was a liar to say so.

Ah, this looking-glass man!
Liar, fool, dreamer, play-actor,
Soldier, dusty drinker of dust—
Ah! he will go with me
Down the dark stairway
When nobody else is looking,
When everybody else is gone.

He locks his elbow in mine,
I lose all—but not him.

## MANUAL SYSTEM

Mary has a thingamajig clamped on her ears
And sits all day taking plugs out and sticking plugs in.
Flashes and flashes—voices and voices
                    calling for ears to pour words in
Faces at the ends of wires asking for other faces
                    at the ends of other wires:
All day taking plugs out and sticking plugs in,
Mary has a thingamajig clamped on her ears.

## PSALM OF THOSE WHO GO FORTH
## BEFORE DAYLIGHT

The policeman buys shoes slow and careful; the teamster
buys gloves slow and careful; they take care of their
feet and hands; they live on their feet and hands.

The milkman never argues; he works alone and no one speaks to him; the city is asleep when he is on the job; he puts a bottle on six hundred porches and calls it a day's work; he climbs two hundred wooden stairways; two horses are company for him; he never argues.

The rolling-mill men and the sheet-steel men are brothers of cinders; they empty cinders out of their shoes after the day's work; they ask their wives to fix burnt holes in the knees of their trousers; their necks and ears are covered with a smut; they scour their necks and ears; they are brothers of cinders.

## SOUP

I saw a famous man eating soup.
I say he was lifting a fat broth
Into his mouth with a spoon.
His name was in the newspapers that day
Spelled out in tall black headlines
And thousands of people were talking about him.

When I saw him,
He sat bending his head over a plate
Putting soup in his mouth with a spoon.

# BIRDS AND BUGS

## LAUGHING CORN

There was a high majestic fooling
Day before yesterday in the yellow corn.

And day after tomorrow in the yellow corn
There will be a high majestic fooling.

The ears ripen in late summer
And come on with a conquering laughter,
Come on with a high and conquering laughter.

The long-tailed blackbirds are hoarse.
One of the smaller blackbirds chitters on a stalk
And a spot of red is on its shoulder
And I never heard its name in my life.

Some of the ears are bursting.
A white juice works inside.
Cornsilk creeps in the end and dangles in the wind.
Always—I never knew it any other way—
The wind and the corn talk things over together.
And the rain and the corn and the sun and the corn
Talk things over together.

Over the road is the farmhouse.
The siding is white and a green blind is slung loose.
It will not be fixed till the corn is husked.
The farmer and his wife talk things over together.

## BUG SPOTS

This bug carries spots on his back.
Last summer he carried these spots.
Now it is spring and he is back here again
With a domino design over his wings.
All winter he has been in a bedroom,
In a hole, in a hammock, hung up, stuck away,
Stashed while the snow blew over
The wind and the dripping icicles,
The tunnels of the frost.
Now he has errands again in a rotten stump.

# PEARL COBWEBS

*from* SMOKE AND STEEL

Pearl cobwebs in the windy rain,
in only a flicker of wind,
are caught and lost and never known again.

A pool of moonshine comes and waits,
but never waits long: the wind picks up
loose gold like this and is gone.

A bar of steel sleeps and looks slant-eyed
on the pearl cobwebs, the pools of moonshine;
sleeps slant-eyed a million years,
sleeps with a coat of rust, a vest of moths,
a shirt of gathering sod and loam.

The wind never bothers . . . a bar of steel.
The wind picks only . . . pearl cobwebs . . . pools of
    moonshine.

## SPRING GRASS

Spring grass, there is a dance to be danced for you.
Come up, spring grass, if only for young feet.
Come up, spring grass, young feet ask you.

Smell of the young spring grass,
You're a mascot riding on the wind horses.
You came to my nose and spiffed me. This is your lucky
    year.

Young spring grass just after the winter,
Shoots of the big green whisper of the year,
Come up, if only for young feet.
Come up, young feet ask you.

## PEOPLE OF THE EAVES,
## I WISH YOU GOOD MORNING

The wrens have troubles like us. The house of a wren will
  not run itself any more than the house of a man.
They chatter the same as two people in a flat where the
  laundry came back with the shirts of another man
  and the shimmy of another woman.

The shirt of a man wren and the shimmy of a woman
wren are a trouble in the wren house. It is this or
something else back of this chatter a spring morning.
Trouble goes so quick in the wren house. Now they are
hopping wren jigs beaten off in a high wren staccato
time.
People of the eaves, I wish you good morning, I wish
you a thousand thanks.

## JUST BEFORE APRIL CAME

The snow piles in dark places are gone.
Pools by the railroad tracks shine clear.
The gravel of all shallow places shines.
A white pigeon reels and somersaults.

Frogs plutter and squdge—and frogs beat the air with a
    recurring thin steel sliver of melody.
Crows go in fives and tens; they march their black feath-
    ers past a blue pool; they celebrate an old festival.
A spider is trying his webs, a pink bug sits on my hand
    washing his forelegs.
I might ask: Who are these people?

# MAROON WITH SILVER FROST

Whispers of maroon came on the little river.
The slashed hill took up the sunset,
Took up the evening star.
The brambles crackled in a fire call
To the beginnings of frost.
"It is almost night," the maroon whispered in widening
    blood rings on the little river.
"It is night," the sunset, the evening star said later over
    the hump of the slashed hill.
"What if it is?" the brambles crackled across the sure
    silver beginnings of frost.

## RAT RIDDLES

There was a gray rat looked at me
with green eyes out of a rathole.

"Hello, rat," I said,
"Is there any chance for me
to get on to the language of the rats?"

And the green eyes blinked at me,
blinked from a gray rat's rathole.

"Come again," I said,
"Slip me a couple of riddles;
there must be riddles among the rats."

And the green eyes blinked at me
and a whisper came from the gray rathole:
"Who do you think you are and why is a rat?
Where did you sleep last night and why do you sneeze
      on Tuesdays? And why is the grave of a rat no
      deeper than the grave of a man?"

And the tail of a green-eyed rat
Whipped and was gone at a gray rathole.

# CRICKET MARCH

As the corn becomes higher
The one shrill of a summer cricket
Becomes two and ten
With a shrilling surer than last month.

As the banners of the corn
Come to their highest flying in the wind,
The summer crickets come to a marching army.

# SPLINTER

The voice of the last cricket
across the first frost
is one kind of good-by.
It is so thin a splinter of singing.

## EVENING WATERFALL

What was the name you called me?—
And why did you go so soon?

The crows lift their caw on the wind,
And the wind changed and was lonely.

The warblers cry their sleepy-songs
Across the valley gloaming,
Across the cattle-horns of early stars.

Feathers and people in the crotch of a treetop
Throw an evening waterfall of sleepy-songs.

What was the name you called me?—
And why did you go so soon?

# SMALL HOMES

The green bug sleeps in the white lily ear.
The red bug sleeps in the white magnolia.
Shiny wings, you are choosers of color.
You have taken your summer bungalows wisely.

# NIGHT

## MILK-WHITE MOON,
## PUT THE COWS TO SLEEP

Milk-white moon, put the cows to sleep.
Since five o'clock in the morning,
Since they stood up out of the grass,
Where they slept on their knees and hocks,
They have eaten grass and given their milk
And eaten grass again and given milk,
And kept their heads and teeth at the earth's face.
    Now they are looking at you, milk-white moon.
    Carelessly as they look at the level landscapes,
    Carelessly as they look at a pail of new white milk,
    They are looking at you, wondering not at all, at all.
    If the moon is the skim face top of a pail of milk,
    Wondering not at all, carelessly looking.
    Put the cows to sleep, milk-white moon,
    Put the cows to sleep.

# GOOD NIGHT

Many ways to spell good night.

Fireworks at a pier on the Fourth of July spell it with
  red wheels and yellow spokes.
They fizz in the air, touch the water and quit.
Rockets make a trajectory of gold-and-blue and then
  go out.

Railroad trains at night spell with a smokestack mush-
  rooming a white pillar.

Steamboats turn a curve in the Mississippi crying in a
  baritone that crosses lowland cottonfields to a razor-
  back hill.

It is easy to spell good night.
  Many ways to spell good night.

# LUMBER YARD POOLS AT SUNSET

The rain pools in the old lumber yard
change as the sky changes.

No sooner do lightfoot sunset maroons
cross the west than they cross the
rain pools too.

So now every blue has a brother
and every singing silver a sister.

# SUMMER STARS

Bend low again, night of summer stars.
So near you are, sky of summer stars,
So near, a long arm man can pick off stars,
Pick off what he wants in the sky bowl,
So near you are, summer stars,
So near, strumming, strumming,
So lazy and hum-strumming.

## NOCTURN CABBAGE

Cabbages catch at the moon.
It is late summer, no rain, the pack of the soil cracks
    open, it is a hard summer.
In the night the cabbages catch at the moon, the leaves
    drip silver, the rows of cabbages are series of little
    silver waterfalls in the moon.

## SLEEPYHEADS

Sleep is a maker of makers. Birds sleep. Feet cling
to a perch. Look at the balance. Let the legs loosen,
the backbone untwist, the head go heavy over, the
whole works tumbles a done bird off the perch.

Fox cubs sleep. The pointed head curls round into
hind legs and tail. It is a ball of red hair. It is a muff
waiting. A wind might whisk it in the air across
pastures and rivers, a cocoon, a pod of seeds. The
snooze of the black nose is in a circle of red hair.

Old men sleep. In chimney corners, in rocking chairs,
at wood stoves, steam radiators. They talk and forget
and nod and are out of talk with closed eyes. For-
getting to live. Knowing the time has come useless

for them to live. Old eagles and old dogs run and fly in the dreams.

Babies sleep. In flannels the papoose faces, the bambino noses, and dodo, dodo the song of many matushkas. Babies—a leaf on a tree in the spring sun. A nub of a new thing sucks the sap of a tree in the sun, yes a new thing, a what-is-it? A left hand stirs, an eyelid twitches, the milk in the belly bubbles and gets to be blood and a left hand and an eyelid. Sleep is a maker of makers.

# SMOKE ROSE GOLD

The dome of the capitol looks to the Potomac river.
    Out of haze over the sunset,
    Out of a smoke rose gold:
One star shines over the sunset.
Night takes the dome and the river, the sun and the
    smoke rose gold,
The haze changes from sunset to star.
The pour of a thin silver struggles against the dark.
A star might call: It's a long way across.

## EARLY MOON

The baby moon, a canoe, a silver papoose canoe, sails and
  sails in the Indian west.
A ring of silver foxes, a mist of silver foxes, sit and sit
  around the Indian moon.
One yellow star for a runner, and rows of blue stars for
  more runners, keep a line of watchers.

O foxes, baby moon, runners, you are the panel of mem-
ory, fire-white writing tonight of the Red Man's
dreams.
Who squats, legs crossed and arms folded, matching its
look against the moon-face, the star-faces, of the
West?
Who are the Mississippi Valley Ghosts, of copper fore-
heads, riding wiry ponies in the night?—no bridles,
love-arms on the pony necks, riding in the night a
long old trail?
Why do they always come back when the silver foxes sit
around the early moon, a silver papoose, in the Indian west?

# SUNSETS

There are sunsets who whisper a good-by.
It is a short dusk and a way for stars.
Prairie and sea rim they go level and even
And the sleep is easy.

There are sunsets who dance good-by.
They fling scarves half to the arc,
To the arc then and over the arc.
Ribbons at the ears, sashes at the hips,
Dancing, dancing good-by. And here sleep
Tosses a little with dreams.

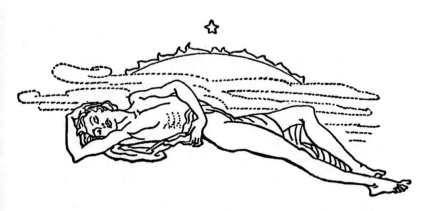

# VALLEY SONG

The sunset swept
To the valley's west, you remember.

The frost was on.
A star burnt blue.
We were warm, you remember,
And counted the rings on a moon.

The sunset swept
To the valley's west
And was gone in a big dark door of stars.

# END THOUGHTS

## HAPPINESS

I asked professors who teach the meaning of life to tell
    me what is happiness.
And I went to famous executives who boss the work of
    thousands of men.
They all shook their heads and gave me a smile as though
    I was trying to fool with them.
And then one Sunday afternoon I wandered out along
    the Desplaines River
And I saw a crowd of Hungarians under the trees with
    their women and children and a keg of beer and an
    accordion.

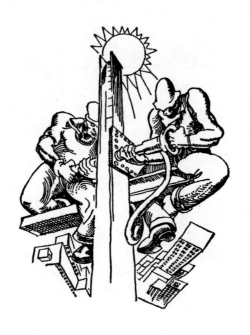

## PRAYERS OF STEEL

Lay me on an anvil, O God.
Beat me and hammer me into a crowbar.
Let me pry loose old walls.
Let me lift and loosen old foundations.

Lay me on an anvil, O God.
Beat me and hammer me into a steel spike.
Drive me into the girders that hold a skyscraper together.
Take red-hot rivets and fasten me into the central girders.
Let me be the great nail holding a skyscraper through
　　blue nights into white stars.

# TRINITY PEACE

The grave of Alexander Hamilton is in Trinity yard at
the end of Wall Street.

The grave of Robert Fulton likewise is in Trinity yard
where Wall Street stops.

And in this yard stenogs, bundle boys, scrubwomen, sit
on the tombstones, and walk on the grass of graves,
speaking of war and weather, of babies, wages and
love.

An iron picket fence . . . and streaming thousands
along Broadway sidewalks . . . straw hats,
faces, legs . . . a singing, talking, hustling river
. . . down the great street that ends with a Sea.

. . . easy is the sleep of Alexander Hamilton.
. . . easy is the sleep of Robert Fulton.
. . . easy are the great governments and the great
steamboats.

# DO YOU WANT AFFIDAVITS?

There's a hole in the bottom of the sea.
> Do you want affidavits?
There's a man in the moon with money for you.
> Do you want affidavits?
There are ten dancing girls in a sea-chamber off Nantucket waiting for you.
There are tall candles in Timbuctoo burning penance for you.
There are—anything else?
Speak now—for now we stand amid the great wishing windows—and the law says we are free to be wishing all this week at the windows.
Shall I raise my right hand and swear to you in the monotone of a notary public? this is "the truth, the whole truth, and nothing but the truth."

*Books by Carl Sandburg*
*available in paperback editions*
*from Harcourt Brace Jovanovich, Inc.*

ABE LINCOLN GROWS UP

EARLY MOON

PRAIRIE-TOWN BOY

ROOTABAGA STORIES. PART I

ROOTABAGA STORIES. PART II: ROOTABAGA PIGEONS

Printed in the United States
5095